Wonderful and Wispy

This wreath spreads warmth and elegance throughout any room. The unique grapevine twigs give this wreath a style like no other.

Cozy rust, golden yellow and burgundy flowers wrap you in an organic quiet that will turn your home into a peaceful retreat.

SIZE: 24" x 24"

MATERIALS:
24" Wispy Twig Grapevine Wreath
Flowers: 2 Brown Gladioli (14" long blooms)
2 Rust Peonies (6" blooms)
1 Dark Rust Dahlia (4" bloom)
Stems: 2 Golden Yellow Wild Saffron (6" long blooms)
2 Rust Wildflowers stems (8" long blooms)
1 Huckleberry stem
1 Sage Green dried flower stem (1" long blooms)
1 Golden Yellow Dried Wildflower (3" blooms)
2 Crabapple sprays
Glue gun
Glue sticks

INSTRUCTIONS:

TIP: Glue the flowers going in the same direction as the twigs coming out from the center of the wreath.

Glue 1 Peony in the bottom center of the wreath. Glue the second Peony to the left of the first Peony. • Glue the Dahlia to the upper left of the second Peony.

Glue 1 Yellow Wild Saffron flower to the right of the Peonies along the inside of the wreath; glue the other Wild Saffron coming out from the top center of the wreath with the bloom going to the left.

Glue a Brown Gladiola to the right of the first Peony along the bottom edge of the wreath. Glue the other Gladiola above the first one.

Glue 2 long Rust blooms to hang into the center of the wreath. Glue another at the bottom of the wreath between the two Peonies, and the last one on the right outside edge between the two Gladioli.

Fill in the rest of the wreath with the remaining greenery and flowers.

Use a Wispy Twig Grapevine Wreath as the Base to Make Any Wreath Special.

December

Present your guests with a festive welcome. This gorgeous wreath glitters with traditional holiday spirit in sumptuous reds, glorious greens, and sparkling gold.

SIZE: 18" x 18"
MATERIALS:
18" Evergreen wreath
Wire-edged ribbon:
- 4 yds Red $2\frac{1}{2}$" wide
- 4 yds Gold $1\frac{1}{2}$" wide

Picks:
- 3 metallic Red feather
- 1 large Red berry
- 3 small Red berry cluster
- 8 Gold, 6 Red
- 5 combination picks of Red, Green, and Gold

2 long Red/Gold berry stems
2 long Red berry stems
24 gauge wire
Glue gun, Glue sticks

INSTRUCTIONS:

Glue 1 feather pick on each outside edge towards the bottom. Glue the 3rd feather pick in the center of the wreath off to one side.

Glue the long Red and Gold berry stems on either side of the wreath, bending as needed. • Cut the long berry stems in the center to make 3 stems. Glue these alongside the feathers. • Starting at the bottom of the wreath, start gluing the picks in place. Once you get to the top of the wreath, stop, leaving a few picks to fill in after the bow is placed.

Create the bow with the Red ribbon on top of the Gold and make a center loop, with 4 loops on each side. The side loops should be $4\frac{1}{2}$" - 5" long. Wire the bow to the wreath. Glue as necessary, then fill in any empty spaces around the bow with leftover picks.

Elegant Holly Days

Seasons Greetings! Your house will be fit for royalty with this wreath adorning your home. Rich Burgundy and Gold colors paired with the evergreen of the wreath impress with simple elegance.

SIZE: 18" x 18"
MATERIALS:
18" evergreen wreath
5 yds Burgundy/Gold $2\frac{1}{2}$" wire-edged ribbon
Picks:
- 1 violin
- 2 Burgundy large crystallized berry
- 2 Burgundy small berry spray
- 2 Green berry with large leaves
- 2 Burgundy glitter present
- 2 medium Burgundy berry
- 2 small Burgundy berry cluster
- 3 small Gold berry cluster

6 small Burgundy ball ornaments
1 stem of 3 velvet Burgundy 4" Poinsettias
1 long Gold berry spray
24 gauge wire
Glue gun and Glue sticks

INSTRUCTIONS:

Make a 4-loop bow. The loops on the outside are $5\frac{1}{2}$" long and the 3 inner loops are 5" long. Leave 25" tails hanging from each side of the bow. Attach the bow at the top of the wreath 4" left of the top center of the wreath. Loop tails along the sides of the wreath and wrap with pieces of the evergreen wreath in two places on each side to hold in place and give the looped look.

Cut 3 Poinsettias from the stem and glue them individually in place slightly off center to the right.

Glue the violin pick in the center right of the wreath. Glue the 2 Burgundy glitter berry spray picks coming out from either side of the top of the bow. Glue the 2 Burgundy crystallized large berry picks coming out from either side of the bottom of the bow. Glue the rest of the picks and berries in place.

Cut the long Gold berry spray into several pieces and use as filler.

Basics of Wreath Design

4 Main Things When Creating a Wreath

Size: Wreaths come in a variety of sizes. Determine where you plan to hang the wreath, then choose the size that best fits your space. The size of the wreath will determine the number and the size of flowers to purchase. Also, choose a ribbon width that is in proportion with the wreath size.

Style: The style of the wreath determines the theme. Are you planning to create a Christmas wreath or a Spring wreath? This will determine whether you will need an evergreen wreath or a grapevine wreath to start. Will your wreath be an indoor or outdoor wreath? This will determine the types of flowers and ribbon you will use. Dried flowers do not work as well on outdoor wreaths and thin ribbon tends to lose its shape when placed outdoors. You also need to consider the types of flowers that will work well with your style of wreath. For a Christmas wreath, poinsettias are a good choice. For a spring wreath, Hydrangea work well.

Color: Understanding the style can help with color choice. If you chose a Christmas wreath, your colors would most likely be red and green. If you are creating a wreath for the interior of your home, you will want to choose colors that complement the colors in the room.

Layout: There are endless choices when it comes to the layout of your wreath. Some of the more important considerations are: Will your wreath have a bow? Will the flowers cover the entire wreath or just a portion? Will your wreath be symmetrical with everything even on both sides, or will it be asymmetrical with the flowers off center or on the side?

The best way to determine the layout of your wreath is to place the flowers on the wreath without gluing or cutting them until the layout is pleasing to you. It is always a good idea to have small flowers or greenery to fill in any empty looking spaces once everything else has been glued in place.

How to Care for Your Wreath

To dust your wreath, use a small vacuum or a vacuum attachment as long as it doesn't pull too hard on the flowers. You can also use a dusting cloth or a clean, slightly damp washcloth. Be cautious if dried flowers are included in the wreath. These can easily break off and must be dusted with care.

To prepare your wreath for storage, stuff the loops of the bow with tissue paper to maintain the shape. Then place the wreath in a wreath box or large plastic bag or attach it to a hanger with wire and cover it with a plastic bag. Store your wreath in a place that is neither too hot nor too cold.

See instructions for 'The Basic Bow' on page 11.

Wreaths come in an array of styles and sizes. Straw, eucalyptus, pine and grapevine are the most popular types.

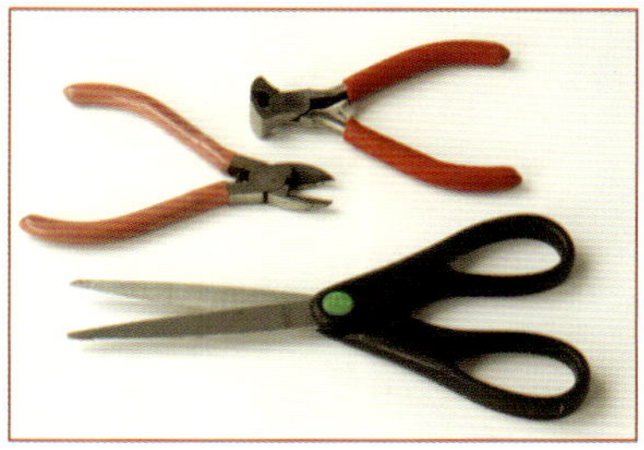

Heavy-Duty Wire Cutters are used for cutting floral wire and trimming down the ends of floral stems. Use sharp scissors to cut ribbon to form bows.

Wire comes in a wide assortment of gauges (the higher the number the thinner the wire). Use a lighter gauge wire to secure bunches of flowers together and for bows. Use a heavy gauge wire for extending the stems of flowers.

Ribbon comes in a variety of styles, textures, colors and widths. Wired ribbon is excellent for making bows in that, once it is shaped, it is more likely to retain its form.

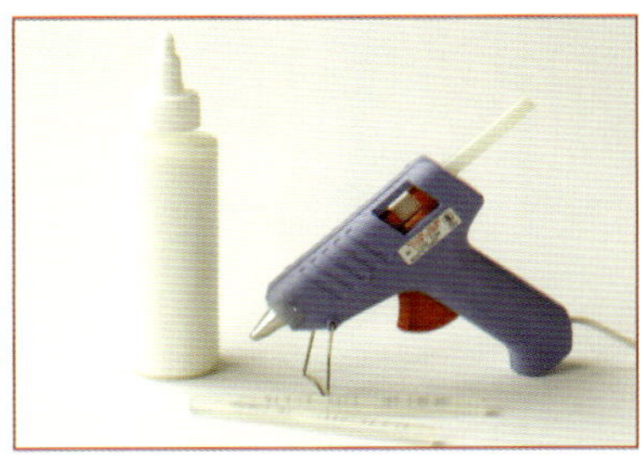

A Glue Gun will allow placement of flowers into small delicate areas and gives a quicker set time of the glue to insure more accurate placement.

Silk Flowers come in a variety of choices. They are made from different types of materials: silk, polyester, etc. Most have flexible stems that are easy to bend and trim.

SIZE: 18" x 18"

MATERIALS:
18" grapevine wreath
3 yds Ivory $1\frac{1}{2}$" wire-edged sheer ribbon
8" tall wooden cross
Gold acrylic paint
2 Eucalyptus sprays
Flowers:
- 1 Green Hydrangea ($5\frac{1}{2}$" bloom)
- 1 Pink Hydrangea ($5\frac{1}{2}$" bloom)
- 2 Green Panicle Hydrangea (7" long blooms)
- 2 Pink Roses ($4\frac{1}{2}$" blooms)
- 1 Pink Rose Stem ($2\frac{1}{2}$" blooms)
- 1 Pink Alstroemeria/ Peruvian Lily stem ($1\frac{1}{2}$" blooms)

24 gauge wire
Glue gun and Glue sticks

April

Celebrate the spirit of Easter by displaying a gorgeous wreath bedecked in triumphant Spring colors.

INSTRUCTIONS:

Paint the cross. Let dry. • Glue the cross into the bottom center of the wreath.

Glue pieces of Eucalyptus and Peruvian Lily on each side of the cross.

Make a bow with two 4" loops on each side and no center loop. Attach to the wreath below the cross and push all loops up towards the cross. • Glue the Green Hydrangea on the bottom of the wreath just to the left of center. Glue the Pink Hydrangea to the right of the Green one. Glue a Rosebud between the 2 Hydrangea at the top. Glue a $2\frac{1}{2}$" Rose and some Peruvian Lily between the 2 Hydrangea at the bottom. Glue a $4\frac{1}{2}$" Pink Rose to the left of the Green Hydrangea, and another to the right of the Pink Hydrangea. Glue 2 Green Panicle Hydrangea, one on each side, above the large Pink Roses.

Glue some Eucalyptus and Lilies on each side under the $4\frac{1}{2}$" Pink Roses.

Make 3 bows with no center loop and one 4" loop on each side. Attach one at the bottom center of the wreath under the $2\frac{1}{2}$" Pink Rose. Attach the others on each side approximately 8" up from the bottom center of the wreath.

Fill in as desired with the remaining flowers and greenery.

SIZE: 18" x 18"

MATERIALS:

18" grapevine wreath

3 yds White 2" wide wire-edged ribbon

Flowers:

- 2 White berry stems
- 1 White Gladiola (12" long bloom)
- 1 White Hyacinth (7" long bloom)
- 1 White Hydrangea ($5\frac{1}{2}$" bloom)
- 2 White Wisteria stems ($6\frac{1}{2}$" long blooms)
- 1 Large White Rose with Pink tips ($4\frac{1}{2}$" bloom)
- 2 White Rose Stems with Pink tips (1"-3" blooms)

24 gauge wire

Glue gun and Glue sticks

INSTRUCTIONS:

Make a bow with 4 loops 4"-5" on each side of the center loop and 7" tails. Attach the bow just to the right of the bottom center.

Glue the Gladiola along the right inside of the wreath behind the bow. Glue the Hyacinth to the right of the bow. Glue the large Rose between the Gladiola and the Hyacinth. Glue a Rose from the Rose stem between the tails of the bow, and two to the left of the bow. Glue the Hydrangea to the left of the two Roses. Glue a Rose and Rosebud coming out from the top of the Hydrangea.

Fill in the spaces with the Rosebuds, Wisteria, leaves, and berries.

June

June is the month for weddings, but it can also symbolize a new beginning, a fresh start, a time of renewal. This wreath can celebrate any or all of those things while bringing natural beauty to your home.

SIZE: 18" x 18"
MATERIALS:
18" grapevine wreath
1½ yds ⅞" Black ribbon
1½ yds ⅞" wide Orange ribbon
Wood 5/16" dowel rod
3 paper mache balls
Acrylic paint (Orange, Brown)
1 pkg Chenille stems (Green, Black)
Black 2" pom pom
2 wiggle eyes 7mm
Flowers:
- 1 Black Baby's Breath stem (½" blooms)
- 2 Black Eucalyptus sprays
- 2 Orange Ranunculus stems (2½" bloom)
- 2 Orange and Yellow Spider Daisy Sprays (2½" blooms)
- 4 Orange carnations (4" bloom)
- 1 Golden Yellow Dried Wildflower stem (3" blooms)

24 gauge wire
Glue gun and Glue sticks

INSTRUCTIONS:

Spider: Cut 4 pieces of Black chenille stem 5" long. Bend them slightly in the center. Tie a piece of thread into a tight knot around the center of the pom pom and leave a long piece of string hanging from the top. This string will be used to tie the spider to the wreath and suspend the spider in the center. Glue the bent center of the chenille stem to the bottom center of the Black pom pom. Let the glue dry. Shape the legs as desired. Glue the eyes in place.

Pumpkins: Make a hole in the top of the paper mache balls large enough to fit the dowel rod. Paint the paper mache balls with Orange paint. Paint faces on the Orange balls with Brown paint. Cut three 2" pieces of dowel rod and paint them Brown. • Wrap Green chenille stems around a pencil 3-4 times to make a spiral and cut off the excess. Make 3 spirals. • Form leaves out of the Green chenille stems by bending into a football shape. Make 3 leaves. • For each pumpkin, glue one end of a chenille spiral and a painted dowel into the hole. Let the glue dry. Glue a leaf onto the pumpkin next to the stem.

Assembly: Glue 3 pumpkins into the bottom center of the wreath. • Make a Black ribbon 3-loop bow with no center loop. The loops should be 3½" long. Attach that bow to the bottom of the wreath below the pumpkins. • Make an Orange ribbon 3-loop bow with 3" long loops. Attach this bow on top of the Black bow. • Glue a Carnation on each side of the bow. Glue an Orange Ranunculus and a Dried Yellow Wildflower on the outside edges of both Carnations. Glue another Orange Carnation going up each side. • Fill in the remainder of the spaces with the Black Eucalyptus, Black Baby's Breath, Yellow and Orange Spider Daisies and greenery from the flowers. • Attach the pom pom spider to the top center of the wreath with the long string.

October

Invite all the neighborhood ghosts and goblins to your door with this Halloween wreath. Cute jack-o-lanterns and a google-eyed spider are a treat for anyone who sees it.

SIZE: 18" x 18"

MATERIALS:

18" grapevine wreath
Raffia
Flowers:
- 1 Cattail stem with grass (4½" long)
- 2 Sunflower stems (4½"-5" blooms)
- 1 Poppy stem (2" blooms)
- 3 Orange large Chrysanthemums (4½" blooms)
- 1 Rust small Chrysanthemum stem (2" blooms)
- 1 Miniature Alstroemeria/Peruvian Lily bush (½"-1" blooms)
- 1 small Ivory Daisy bush (1"-2" blooms)

1 wood and metal turkey
1 set of 3 miniature dried corn
24 gauge wire
Glue gun and Glue sticks

INSTRUCTIONS:

Glue the turkey in the center of the wreath, slightly to the left.

Untie the set of 3 dried corns and wire them individually onto the bottom center of the wreath. • Tie a shoelace bow with the raffia and glue into place over the tops of the dried corns.

Glue a large Orange Chrysanthemum below the bow and between the corn. Glue 2 Sunflowers on either side of the bow. Glue two Cattails in the center of the wreath behind the turkey on the left side. Glue one Cattail along the right side of the wreath behind the Sunflowers. Glue stems from the Alstroemeria bush and Poppies alongside the Cattails.

Fill in the spaces with the remaining flowers.

November

Harvest and Thanksgiving go hand in hand. Create a seasonal wreath that overflows with the rich bounty of a fruitful Earth with fabulous fall foliage and the traditional turkey. You can proudly display this wreath for all of your friends and family.

February

Love is in the air! Red and pink roses on a heart-shaped wreath add a touch of romance that is perfect for the Valentine season.

SIZE: 14" x 14"

MATERIALS:

14" Heart-shaped grapevine wreath
2 yds Pink and Red striped 1½" wide wire-edged ribbon
Flowers:
- 3 Pink Roses (3½" bloom size)
- 3 Red Roses (3½" bloom size)
- 2 stems White Daisies (bloom sizes on the stem include ½", 1", and 2")
- 1 stem White Baby's Breath

24 gauge wire
Glue gun and Glue sticks

INSTRUCTIONS:

Make a bow with 1 loop 3" long on each side of the center loop leaving 4" tails. Attach the bow at the top center of the wreath.

Make 2 bows without a center loop that have 1 loop on each side. Attach 1 on each side 4" from the bottom center of the wreath. Cut a Red Rose stem 4" long and glue it in the bottom center standing up into the center of the wreath.

Glue 2 Pink Roses slightly lower on each side of the Red Rose. Glue a Red Rose to the bottom center. Glue a Pink Rose on the right side 3½" up from the nearest Pink Rose. Glue a Red Rose on the left side 3½" up from the nearest Pink Rose.

Fill in with Baby's Breath, Daisies, and leaves from the Roses.

May

April showers bring May flowers and this wreath shows how beautiful those flowers can be. The rich tones of the Peony, Hyacinth, and Carnations, along with the magnificent large blooms, proclaim an eager expectation of Summer.

SIZE: 18" x 18"

MATERIALS:
18" grapevine wreath
4 yds striped 1½" wide wire-edged ribbon
Flowers:
- 2 Hot Pink Carnations (4" blooms)
- 2 Magenta Carnation stems (2½" blooms)
- 2 Hot Pink Peony stems (3½" blooms)
- 2 Yellow Peony stems (3½" blooms)
- 1 Light Pink Peony stems (3½" blooms)
- 2 Purple Hyacinth (blooms 5" long)
- 2 Blue Hyacinth (blooms 5" long)
- 2 Magenta Hyacinth (blooms 5" long)
- 2 Ivory Hyacinth (blooms 5" long)

24 gauge wire
Glue gun and Glue sticks

INSTRUCTIONS:

Make a bow with 3 loops 3½" long on either side of the center loop with 44" tails. Attach the bow to the top center of the wreath.

Glue a Light Pink Peony above the center of the bow. Glue a Hot Pink and Yellow Peony bud below the bow. Glue a Purple Hyacinth to the right and a Magenta Hyacinth to the left of the Peony buds. Glue the Hot Pink Carnations on both sides of the bow. Glue the Yellow and Hot Pink Peony flowers next to the Carnations.

Fill in the rest with the remaining flowers.

Loop the bow tails through the flowers, gluing the loops in place on the wreath. Trim the ends and let them hang out from the bottom of the flowers.

Basic Bow

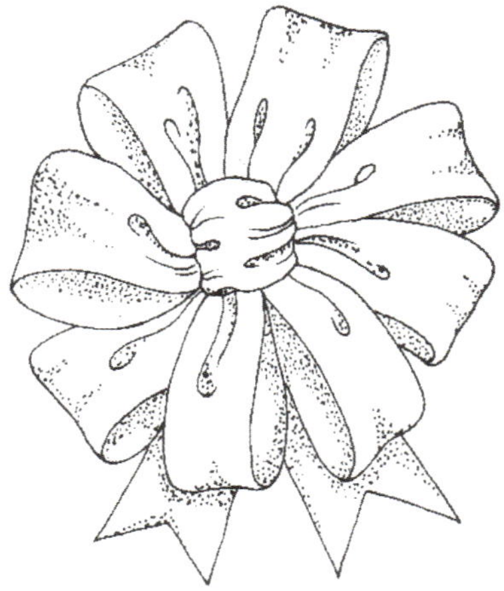

Check instructions for length of ribbon and length of bow. Cut ribbon following the instructions. Cut a wire long enough to tie the bow and secure it to the wreath.

If the ribbon has a right side and wrong side, twist the bottom part of the ribbon so the right side can be seen.

TIP: Sometimes a design calls for a bow without a center loop because flowers will be added and the loop would get in the way. Follow the instructions for the Basic Bow, eliminating the step for the center loop.

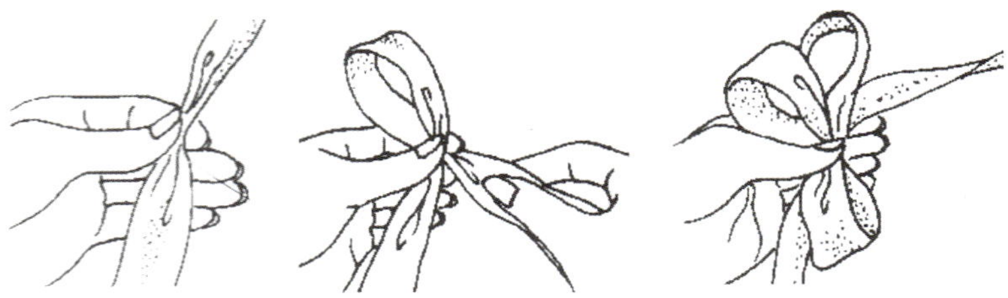

1. Pinch the ribbon between your thumb and forefinger.
2. Make a half twist with the ribbon to keep the right side facing you.
3. Bring the ribbon up and back forming a second loop

4. Twist again and form a third loop on the same side as your thumb.
5. Twist again and form a fourth loop opposite the third loop.
6. Make a center loop by bringing the ribbon toward you - up, over your thumb.

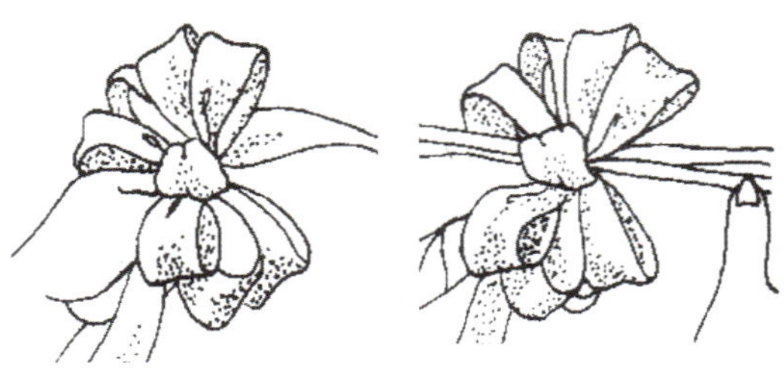

7. Continue making four more loops as instructed in steps 2-6.
8. Insert the length of wire through the small center loop. Bring the ends of wire to back of bow and twist ends together firmly, securing the bow.

SIZE: 12" x 12"

MATERIALS:

12" Evergreen wreath

4 yds White 1½" wide wire-edged ribbon

Flowers:

- Ice stem pick
- 3 Silver feather picks
- 3 Jingle bell picks
- 2 Silver Holly picks
- 2 Silver-covered greenery picks
- 2 Silver berry stems
- 1 White berry cluster pick
- 2 White Poinsettia stems with Silver glitter

1 pkg of snow-covered dried branches

24 gauge wire

Glue gun and Glue sticks

INSTRUCTIONS:

Make a bow with 6 loops on each side of the center loop with 25" tails. The loops are 2½"-3¾" long.

Attach the bow to the wreath a little to the right of center. Loop the ribbon tails along the side of the wreath and wrap a piece of the evergreen from the wreath around the ribbon tails in 2 places on each side to secure the tail loops.

Glue a Silver feather pick in the center of the wreath to the left side and the Ice stem pick in the center middle of the wreath. Glue a Silver-covered greenery pick in the middle right of the wreath.

Cut some Poinsettias from the stem, glue them in front of the Silver-covered greenery. Glue a jingle bell pick to the left of the White Poinsettias. Glue a Silver Holly pick to the left of the jingle bell pick. Glue another Silver Holly pick under the White Poinsettias. Glue another bunch of the White Poinsettias under the jingle bells. Glue the White berry cluster pick under the second Silver Holly pick. Glue 2 feathers coming out from the bottom sides of the wreath. • Cut the Silver berry stems and glue some of the berries over the 2 feathers on the sides of the wreath. Glue more berries coming out from around the bow. Cut pieces of the snow-covered branches and glue them to stick out from the sides.

Glue jingle bell picks on each side of the wreath where the first ribbon tail loops attach to the wreath. Fill in the rest of the wreath with the remaining picks, berries, flowers, and branches.

January

What better way to ring in the New Year than with this Silver and White wreath with jingle bells! Dried stems give the appearance of snow.

No doubt... Old Man Winter is here.

SIZE: 18" x 18"
MATERIALS:
18" grapevine wreath
7 yds of 1½" Gold wire-edged ribbon
Flowers:
3 Green Hydrangea flowers with Gold edges (6" blooms)
2 White Hydrangea flowers with Gold edges (6" blooms)
1 stem of small Gold flowers (½" blooms)
24 gauge wire
Glue gun and Glue sticks

March

Bring the Luck of the Irish to your door with a bit o' the green. This wreath gives the appearance that a pot of gold has been beautifully drizzled with lovely flowers. What a fabulous way to celebrate St. Patrick's Day.

INSTRUCTIONS:

Make a bow with 4 loops 3"-3½" long on each side of the center loop and 20" tails. Attach this bow just left of the center top. Leave the tails dangling for now.

Make a 2nd bow with 5 loops 3"-3½" long on each side of the center loop and 14" tails. Attach this bow just right of the center bottom of the wreath. Leave the tails dangling.

Glue 1 of the Green Hydrangea to the left of the bottom bow. Glue the other 2 Green Hydrangea on each side of the top bow. • Glue a White Hydrangea to the left of the top bow and another above the bottom bow. Pull the tails from the bows under the Hydrangea and have them come out from the sides of the flowers. Loop the ends of the ribbon under a piece of the grapevine wreath and glue in place. Trim the ribbon tails.

Glue leaves from the Hydrangea stems under the flowers. • Cut pieces of the Gold flowers, glue them so that they stick out from around the flowers and bow. Cut two 12" pieces of ribbon, glue the ends under each side of the bottom Hydrangea. Loop ribbons under pieces of the wreath in the center and glue in place. Trim the tails as desired.

SIZE: 18" x 18"

MATERIALS:

18" straw wreath

6 yds of Red-White-Blue 1½" wide wire-edged ribbon

Flowers:

- 2 Red chrysanthemum stems (4" bloom size)
- 1 White Alstroemeria/ Peruvian Lily stem (1½"-2" bloom sizes)
- 1 Blue Alstroemeria/ Peruvian Lily stem (1½"-2" bloom sizes)
- 2 Blue Hyacinth stem (blooms 5" long)
- 1 Red Miniature Rose stem (½"-1" bloom sizes)
- 1 White Wild Daisy stem (1" bloom size)
- 2 White Aster stems (½" blooms; 11" long)
- 1 Grassy greenery stem (greenery is 10" long)

24 gauge wire

Glue gun and Glue sticks

July

Fireworks, brass bands, apple pie, and friends!

Capture the spirit of an Independence Day county fair with this patriotic wreath. What a wonderful way to show your American pride.

INSTRUCTIONS:

Wrap ribbon around the wreath leaving 3" of straw showing between each wrap of ribbon. Glue the ends in place on the back of the wreath.

Make a bow with 4 loops 4"-5" long on each side of the center loop with 10" tails. Attach the bow just to the right of center on the bottom of the wreath.

Glue a Red Chrysanthemum on each side of the bow and 1 above the middle of the bow. Glue 1 more to stand 7" in the center of the wreath. Glue the two smaller Chrysanthemum blooms to the left of the tallest Chrysanthemum. Glue the Blue Alstroemeria behind the Chrysanthemums so that the tallest part touches the top inside of the wreath. Spread the Blue Alstroemeria stems apart. • Cut the Hyacinths from the stems, glue 1 on each side of the Chrysanthemums beside the bow. Glue another Hyacinth below the tall Chrysanthemum that is in the center of the wreath.

Fill in the spaces with the rest of the flowers.

SIZE: 18" x 18"

MATERIALS:

18" grapevine wreath
3 yds of Yellow 1½" wire-edged ribbon
3 yds of Blue gingham ⅝" wide ribbon
1 Yellow visor with sunglasses for dolls
Wood letters
Flowers:
- 2 Yellow Jumbo Gerbera Daisies (6½" blooms)
- 1 Ranunculus Spray stem (2"-2½" blooms)
- 2 Blue Daisy stems (2½" blooms)
- 1 Blue Bachelor Button stem (1½" blooms)
- 1 Yellow Baby's Breath stem (½" blooms)

Acrylic paint (Yellow, Blue)
24 gauge wire
Glue gun and Glue sticks

August

Let The Sunshine In and radiate the warmth of Summer with bright yellow letters and Chrysanthemum flowers that resemble the summer sun. This wreath will surely put a smile on your face every time you see it.

INSTRUCTIONS:

Paint the wooden letters Yellow. Using the handle end of the brush, dip into the Blue paint and make dots on the Yellow letters. • Make a bow with 4 loops 3½" long on each side of the center loop with 9" tails. Attach the bow to the bottom of the wreath just right of the center. • Glue 1 Jumbo Gerbera Daisy coming up from the inside center of the wreath to the right of the bow. Glue the other Jumbo Gerbera Daisy in the inside center of the wreath to the left of the bow.

Cut the Yellow Ranunculus blooms. Put one bloom and a bud coming out from the right side of the bow, the other bloom coming out from the left side of the bow.

Fill in the bottom half of the wreath with the Bachelor Buttons, Blue Daisies, and Yellow Baby's Breath. • Glue the visor on the left side of the top half of the wreath. Glue the painted letters to the right of the visor.

SIZE: 12" x 12"

MATERIALS:

12" straw wreath

8 yds of Ivory $1\frac{1}{2}$" wide ribbon

4 yds of Sheer striped $1\frac{1}{2}$" wide wire-edged ribbon

Flowers:

- 3 yds Aqua Blue shimmer chenille stem
- 1 Ivory Baby's Breath stem
- 1 Hot Pink Zinnia stem

1 Hot Pink feather boa

Pre-painted wood shapes (Green sunglasses, Pink/Yellow hollow heart, Blue-Green striped sandals)

6 wood $\frac{3}{4}$" blocks

5 wood $1\frac{1}{4}$" flat squares

1 Package of foam adhesive backed 'Girl' stickers

24 gauge wire

Glue gun and Glue sticks

For the Girls

No girl's room would be complete without a wreath like this one. The bright colors and girly accessories can be purchased in a variety of colors to customize this wreath for your lucky young lady.

INSTRUCTIONS:

Wrap the straw wreath with Ivory ribbon and then the Pink feather boa. Glue the ends in place on the back of the wreath. Make a sheer ribbon bow with 4 loops on each side of the center loop and 8" tails. The loops should be 3"-4" long.

Cut 11" of Blue chenille stem and shape antennae. Attach the antennae to the back of the bow with the wire, then attach the bow with the antennae just left of the center top of the wreath. • Make a 4 loop bow with no center loop. Loops should be $3\frac{1}{2}$" long with no tail.

Use the Blue chenille stem to make a flower with 5 loops $2\frac{1}{2}$"-3" long. Glue a Zinnia flower to the center of the Blue chenille flower. Glue these flowers to the center of the 4 loop bow. Glue this set to the wreath just to the right of the bottom center.

Glue Baby's Breath behind the bow. Glue the sandals coming out from the left side of the bow. Glue the heart coming out from the upper right side of the bow. Glue the glasses between the bow and flower on the left side. Glue 2 wood blocks together. Repeat for 3 sets. Place the small word stickers onto the top of these block sets. Glue in place.

Place 3 flat wood squares on the back of the 'GIRLS' sticker, then glue Blue chenille stem around the edges. Glue in place on the wreath.

Trim the clear backing from the 'Girls Rock' sticker sheet so that it remains on the sticker part, but is not visible from the front. Wrap string around one of the antennae, then feed the tag through the center of the bow so that it hangs in the middle.

SIZE: 12" x 12"

MATERIALS:
12" straw wreath
9 yds of Baby Blue or Pink 1½" wide weather-resistant satin ribbon
3 yds of acetate 1¼" wide 'It's a Boy' or 'It's a Girl' ribbon
2 yds of Baby Blue or Pink ⅞" wide gingham ribbon
1 White Baby's Breath stem
2 large plastic safety pins
1 large pacifier decoration
24 gauge wire
Glue gun and Glue sticks

For Baby Boy:
1 Baby Blue Bachelor Button stem (1½" blooms)

For Baby Girl:
1 Pink Miniature Rose stem with baby's breath (¾"-1¼" blooms)

New Baby

Thrill a new Mom or Dad!

This wreath is a beautiful way to give a gift that can be used several times. First, use it as a decoration at a baby shower, on a door at home, and baby's room wall. You'll be surprised how easy and affordable it is to make.

INSTRUCTIONS:

Wrap the entire straw wreath with the weather-resistant satin ribbon. • Make an acetate ribbon bow with 5 loops on each side of the center loop and 12" tails for the boy, 15½" tails for the girl. The loops should be 3½"-4" long. Wire the bow to the top center of the wreath. • Glue a Bachelor Button for a boy or a Rose cluster for a girl onto each side of the bow.

Glue a cluster of Baby's Breath above and below each flower. • Tie the gingham ribbon in a knot at the bottom of each safety pin leaving 2"-3" tails. Glue 1 safety pin on each side of the wreath coming out from the flowers.

Glue two 14"-18" lengths of gingham ribbon behind the center bow so that they hang down between the bow tails.

Tie the gingham ribbon in a knot around the handle of the pacifier leaving a 3"-4" tail on one side, and a 1"-2" tail on the other side. Glue the long tail under the bow, but above the tails of the bow so that the pacifier dangles in the center of the wreath.

SIZE: 11" x 17"

MATERIALS:

1 Black 11" x 17" frame
Black chalkboard spray paint
2 yds of Cranberry 1" ribbon
Flowers:
- 2 Sunflowers (4" blooms)
- 1 Huckleberry greenery stem
- 1 Tan Waxflower stem
- 1 Cranberry Wild Daisy stem (1" blooms)
- 1 Cranberry Miniature Rose stem ($\frac{1}{2}$"-1" blooms)

Chalk
24 gauge wire
Glue gun and Glue sticks

INSTRUCTIONS:

Remove the glass, cardboard, and backing from the frame. Discard the glass and apply 2-3 coats of chalkboard paint to the cardboard following the manufacturer's instructions.

Tie a shoelace bow. Make the loops $1\frac{1}{2}$" and leave $7\frac{1}{2}$" tails. Glue the bow in the upper left corner of the frame.

Cut the Huckleberry greenery stems into 4 pieces. Starting from the lower right corner, glue one piece on the right side, one on the bottom, and two in the center of the frame. Glue one piece of the Tan Waxflower stem beside the greenery on the right side and bottom. Glue one more piece of the Waxflower in the center. Fill in with the Cranberry flowers. • Cut five 8" pieces of ribbon and glue them in loops in the lower right corner.

Glue 2 Sunflowers over the ribbon loops.

Insert the cardboard and backing into the frame. Use chalk to write a message on the chalkboard surface.

September

Write your very own personal message to your guests with this wreath variation. A black frame serves as the wreath and the warm, inviting florals provide a very welcoming sight. This will be a fun project and all your friends and family will be impressed with your innovative wreath.